Momma Where is Daddy?

by MONICA AMORES

Illustrations by Marlon at GetYourBookIllustrations

Text and Illustrations copyright © 2022 Monica Amores

Published by SMOT Global Press

All rights reserved.
No part of this publication may be reproduced, distributed, or transmitted in any form or by any means, including photocopying, recording, or other electronic or mechanical methods, without the prior written permission of the publisher, except in the case of brief quotations embodied in reviews and certain other noncommercial uses permitted by copyright law.

The moral right of the author and illustrator has been asserted.

Cover design and illustrations by Marlon at GetYourBookIllustrations
www.getyourbookillustrations.com

Hardback ISBN: 979-8-9856711-0-0
Paperback ISBN: 979-8-9856711-1-7
eBook ISBN: 979-8-9856711-2-4

Library of Congress Control Number: 2022911380

Dedication

Dedicated to my beautiful **SOFI**.

Thank you for always being my baby girl, my pride and joy, who always showed a positive attitude no matter how hard life got for us. I'll never forget your cute little words that encouraged me at my hardest moments:

"Don't worry, Mommy, everything is going to be okay."

You inspired me with your light, and your kind soul encouraged me to become the best version of myself.

Illustrator Dedication

I dedicate this to my Mama, **EVA**, for raising me and my brother while my Papa, Jorge, was working on the other side of the world.

- Marlon of GYBI

Acknowledgment

Thank you God.

Thank you to my support team:

CHRISTINA OBERON for believing in me.

My **MOM** and **ROBERT** (who I consider my dad).

My **BROTHER**, my **SISTERS**, and all the people along the way that came into my life at the right time to help me raise a beautiful young lady.

To **ALL MY SINGLE MOMS**—stay strong, keep working hard for your babies, and never forget that you can do anything you set your mind to!

You and I have a new home now. Daddy is at his house and he can't wait to see you. And guess what? You will get to visit him very soon. So cool, right?! But for right now, Momma is here with you.

Daddy is in the way you laugh when I tickle you. I know you miss the way Daddy tickles you; you will see him very soon. Momma is here right now and we can have twice the fun playing tickle war.

Daddy is in the way you wiggle your cute little nose. I know you miss his Eskimo kisses and the giggles you shared. He will always be your Daddy, ready to giggle at your wiggly nose. Momma and Daddy love you and will be here for you whenever you need us.

Daddy is in the way you kick your ball. You're so good at it! I know you miss playing ball with Daddy, so let's go outside so Momma can play with you!

Daddy is in the way you color; look how beautiful your artwork is! I know you miss Daddy. Next time you see him you can show him everything you colored. I'm sure he'll love that.

Daddy is in the way you swim; look how fast you go! I know you miss pool time with Daddy; next time you see him you can show him all the cool tricks you've learned swimming. He will be so proud of you.

Momma, where is Daddy?

Daddy is in the way you eat all your delicious food. I know you miss eating dinner with Daddy. At Daddy's house, you will have a nice big table just for you and him to enjoy meals together. Now open big, here comes the plane!

Daddy is in the way you smile. When you miss him the most and need another reason to smile, you can call or ask to visit him. He loves to see you because you are so very important to him, it makes him smile too. Now take a selfie with Momma and show me that pretty smile.

Daddy is in the way you brush those shiny teeth you have. I know you miss bedtime with Daddy, but when you go visit him, you can have a new bedtime routine, just you and Daddy. How exciting is that?! Now sing and Dance with Momma!

Daddy is in the way you say your bedtime prayers. Let's pray for Daddy to always have lots of love and kisses like the ones you give Momma and like the ones Momma gives you back.

Momma, where is Daddy?

Daddy is in your heart; every time you think of him, he is there. I want you to remember that Daddy will always love you no matter where he is. Next time you see him, tell him how much you love him. Give him one of those amazing big hugs like the ones you give Momma! I'm sure Daddy would love that. Now come cuddle with Momma.

And I love you, always.

About The Author

MONICA AMORES was born in Quito, Ecuador. She was raised in Los Angeles, California from the age of nine. She became a teenage mom at the age of sixteen to a beautiful little girl named Sofia, who became her whole life and her whole heart. She became a single mom when Sofia was three years old. Monica dedicated her life to raising her daughter as best as she could, making sure she was always a great mom, allowing Sofia to know she was always loved by both her mommy and her daddy. Monica enjoys hanging out with her daughter, spending time with her family, reading, being in nature, making new friends, going to the gym, and eating chocolate chip cookies and croissants.

About The Illustrator

MARLON is a dedicated Filipino Illustrator whose passion is his art. He is a loyal part of GetYourBookIllustrations team.

www.ingramcontent.com/pod-product-compliance
Lightning Source LLC
LaVergne TN
LVHW072116070426
835510LV00002B/73

9789856711117